UTTER

ALSO BY VAHNI CAPILDEO

No Traveller Returns
Person Animal Figure
Undraining Sea
Dark & Unaccustomed Words

VAHNI CAPILDEO

UTTER

PEEPAL TREE

First published in Great Britain in 2013
Peepal Tree Press Ltd
17 King's Avenue
Leeds LS6 1QS
UK

ISBN 13: 9781845232139

Supported using public funding by
ARTS COUNCIL
ENGLAND

CONTENTS

"A flight of steps like birds settling, to bring you all the way here."
— John Hope Welch, *Dreaming Arrival*

i.m. Martin Wylde Carter

UTTER

Night drinks salt water from a bucket, draws
a sleeve from the sea, spills hand across mouth.
Night hands back the bucket to the sailor.
Night, blue-shirted, wades arrhythmically.
Night hurries off uphill.

The sky fires up as if to say what
Tongue swells against teeth as if to say what
The coastline cuts up thick and fortified

Giving the time of day, stranger,
willing this dawn rain down and utter you.

A WORLD

In which the hands of people changed to things like flowers
for which new, uneasy forms of consideration
by which that iron-suited man, foolish and careful,
negotiates crowds, his two wrists bearing red hibiscus
necessarily bruised, a little raised, a little forwards,
a rivelled fountain their corollas accompanying him.

How approach the cockroach-gripped revoker of contracts?
How approach him whose sand crab hands try running askew?
How approach him? or how near the one mobbed by seagulls,
helpless to pull a glove on leaking packets of corn?

Ah whose iced hands disappear, condense, remade droplets...
instant, lasting blister-silk, should he once touch a heart:

STOP, PASSENGER

For Vivek Narayanan

i held out my arms i woke up smiling
i held out my eyes and opened my arms
my eyes held out the arms were awakened
my eyes holding out for an opening
the holding of eyes commencement of arms

Unbeholden, unbidden

as the dog stricken of its fur flees on shipboard
(like a bouquet of roses launched travellerwards from shore)
finding its feet finds no master for mangy days
so mangy days a calendar of gangplanks
gagging and barking a wake of particular salt

Unbidden, unbecoming

as the dog whines and presses up against lifeboats
(cocooned as if hatching monarch butterfly flags)
fledging a fur the wind crisps thin to infancy
the technology of its tail a piece with uselessness
useless with tenderness plumed for a go-nowhere walk

Deterred, abiding

the sea returns to turquoise strung with jets
the shore lines up it is assumed by sight
the shore too much behind the lines too bright
un-sea un-shore waving back each tender
stop passenger it is the jetty night

AUX BIBLIOTHÈQUES AUX ANTILLES

Straightway dropped, still vertical, into a shadow parallel
to other shadows, I appeared to stand above, substantial,
a manifest husk that you, your khaki and navy, address
contentedly.

But look, only one corner is worm-eaten,
my red binding holds most of my yellowed pages together,
you can follow the story which is torn in several places
but in such ways that destruction becomes a second story,
one to love, meddled too with chocolate prints from a baby past.

Good sir, with a long reading list, no translator, and wrong change,
will you pick me?

The risk that you change your mind is mine, not yours:
pick me, and you are irretrievable:
hell is already.
Myself dropped through the floor of myself,
you, broken out of leaf,
mistrustful, pithy, four-dimensioned.
I would be stuck with that.

A lifetime with one who reads me,
by whom I am not seen.

The multifarious integrity of pomegranates.

Sharing a hell with you no king and I an almost queen.

PROCEED WHEN ILLUMINATED

I am not expecting freedom from you:
Anyone
        who sees a lightning rod
        while their spine is building
lifts up their eyes
to the bitter variegation citied
distant
        in the skyline
        that is shoreline
        perfect light
        a version of downpouring
takes a step
        knowing against hoping better
        wind working swift decay
what step they can
        aversion and oncoming.
Proceed when illuminated:
        Freedom.
        And you?
Trees are staggered by lampposts, say landscape,
without jacaranda or aluminium,
landscape vented by a desert mantra.
Tall to that flattening, you are charged with you.

FINDING

It was again transparent waves with cruel undertow
most capable of gaining the irrecoverable;
calculated stepping-in not possible, for they were
breaking all over the place, too close, and stopping to laugh;
and I was plunging in again to warn you: for, stronger,
you'd go out quicker, and more bewildered. That must not be!
But how dark it got, without being late: dark, and entrenched;
while you, emerging alone at the far half of the bay,
showed a face of dismay, as if still caught up in drowning,
and I shocked speechless: for there we were, not having been saved.

COASTAL MAN INDOORS

He has knives in his eyes
two-way knives
knives going in
on the way up the hill
(not us, the ancestors),
knives creeping out
on your introduction.

No, lord, no;
curtains hide their dancers;
room of living marble
teeming, veined and solid,
walls of squared-off air

disarmed,
for in the social moment
see who stepped between,
· slipped a hand beneath his balls
— off in one: it popped
like bladderwrack; eyes bayed,
knives at an ebb hallooed.

The twister stood aside.
The knife-eyed castrate bled
not at all. Recovering,
the room cast his waist
in more marble; he brings
whispering fingers towards
his face; rough magic
riffles the golden dancers
concealed in the missing walls.

INTO DARKNESS / PLUS QUE NOIR
For Attillah Springer

*

Loupgarou

Speak to me though I cannot answer
These days I cannot think and speak when you are near

Dragging great chains of night in his audible walk round the houses
A candled coffin cleaving to his headless neck
Shining with the light of misunderstanding

The loupgarou is a lover
Perennial and never let in

*

Douens

Children you will have me though I never found you
Shades of growing swallowed by oversized sombreros

You go crying through the forest even where land has been cleared
Tearless and whooping hide-and-seek and your feet backwards on their stems
Trickling every cell of possibles that underwent expulsion

The douens dwell on the past
Allured by facelessness we follow

*

Soucouyants

I need you inside me, inside my body as you are inside my mind
Knowledge of you moved me in firing myself, in taking flight

Fireball shedding her skin bloodkisses not just cattle
Her stored skin poisoned by raging neighbours with stamped thighs
She puts on a skin that smelts her, woman of no return

The soucouyant brings desire home
Earth and water make her tomb

IN THE ABSENCE OF LOVE
OR A POSTAL VOTING SYSTEM

a measure of tree overhanging
a soft stone bridge
        (and it feels quicker
        to walk into the city
        than to walk out of the city
        for who lives outside the city
        traipsing with a day's-weight back)
via dereliction
scaffold of winter
when you made your speech
shieldwall respringing
when my speech was received
        (and it is easier
        to push off a building
        or to pull down a building
        easiest to put aside building
        playing draughts in a lightning shack)
forest of dipped reminders
contract of leafmast and paving
fall of our nailed soles

FLANKED WITH SILENCE

The cows discovered in the theatre wear
an abject or an absent-minded air.
Quietly they'd entered, quietly fold
their stilted legs; their grassy stomachs hold
the wonder of free programmes, and a room
that's open on three sides to view. For whom
theatre, if not for cows? Where else such eyes
that, dark and lustrous, graduate like sighs
the effort of eyelashes? Traffic stops
and falls to worshipping cows of the east.
These, our theatre cows, have no such hopes.
They could not pay. Nor can they stay. Their best
(deserving of the spectacle) hauls its tail
slower than pearls o cow immemorial...

*

THE CRITIC IN HIS NATURAL HABITAT

"You seem to be serious about literature. Have you ever considered writing up some of these thoughts of yours? A poet like you could bring a fresh perspective to criticism. People would appreciate that. You needn't worry: they wouldn't expect scholarship. My book came out last year. You don't want me to bore you with that. It's just an in-depth study of darkness and the imagination in the seventeenth century. The seventeenth century might not be your cup of tea. Oh, is that your book? I'm afraid I don't read much contemporary poetry. Will you give me a copy? Only if you have one spare, of course. Sultry photo! I'm never *sure* about books-with-author-photos. The rail station photobooth? Really? You don't write for *The Times Literary Supplement*, do you? Dorina recently did a brilliant review of Tricia's edition of Gussie's translations of Brazilian slum poetry composed in Spanish by a French guy who taught on an art history course here, oh, donkeys' years ago.

I don't remember his name.

He lived in one of those nice houses. Haven't you read them? You read Italian don't you? I'll send you the reference if I can remember to find the time to send it. You wouldn't believe how busy I am. End-of-term exams bang in the middle of barbecue duty. And the family insists on their five days in Cornwall. I'm *so* desperate to get back to my research. Madness! A nightmare! Merciless. But I'd like to See You Again... May I See You Again? (Gracie! Put on the wash, I need my brown corduroy trousers for tomorrow). Sorry.

Oh. You're going away?"

DANCING BEAR SONNET (TRUNCATED)

You've lied through your teeth and it's not a pretty sight.
The fox pulls on his gloves, the poisoner says good night,
the drunk's wife grants him pardon, the drunk necks a drink,
something stirs to gentle life in the kitchen sink;
you say it is not so, no matter what I think,
the drunk's wife beats him up, the drunk's wife needs a drink,
your eyes pinned to my breast are jewelled with regret.

Hand me a stick to poke between the bars you've set.
Walk in the kind of wind that blows dogs inside out.
I too might need a drink. Your skull will do for that.
Always flying off. Nothing to write home about.

THE TASK

It is gross and grotesque. Like the Duomo in Florence. A million liquorice allsorts stuck to the plating of a sea armadillo that grunts itself around in a game of chasetail at low speed.

The only way to see it is to lie down on the street. The skies, velveted with pollution, really improve when viewed as a ground. But then the mother and daughter might step on you.

The daughter should be mother: she walks pretty in pain like a Madonna.

The mother's hair is like the skies: both having achieved blue after a struggle.

The mother gives the task a caption:

"This is not the Cathedral we were looking for."

LA POETESSA

Liberal the college. Fair the lawn. Pontificating by the fountain in the middle of the quad: La Poetessa. Who wishes to hear? She cares not. Slight breezes blow in circles, catching on her words. Waxwings. English her name, English her language, English her absobloomsburylutely witty garments. Yet in her arcane brainpan shudder puddles that are forever Europe. Ewig. Earwig. The book-worm tunnels erotically, spiralling through the silver marshes rife with synaptic missed connexions. Severed segments call out to one another, mateless, growing (with resignation) a head at either end. Don't think she can't take a joke...The crane perches on one leg. Hunch. Balance. Symbol. Derived.

FOR Z., AT THE END OF TERM

A new insanity is setting in, I've noticed.
Walking around, looking relaxed, are those without conscience,
only those, among my colleagues.
For the first time
after so many years, I'm not happy with my job;
I was happy; now I'm one of those: I'm unhappy.
I'm thinking of leaving. There's nothing wrong with the city.
I'm thinking of leaving. But where should I go?
It's strange you should say that.
I almost went there
years ago.

THE GOOD COLLEAGUE

I would like a mint. I usually keep mints. Where are the mints? Oh, how good, I have found the mints! Would you like a mint? Here, have a mint. I am having a mint. There is another person, who is friendly, who is having a mint. There was a friendly transaction involving a mint.

All is temporarily right with the world.

THE DRIP

Cheese is in his blood. He is pale and sweats like a cheese. Some invertebrates breathe via spiracles, a rattle of tiny holes along their sides, a scale of inaudibility. The cheese: as it sweats, does it breathe? Disproportion appears between the porosity of the surface and the pearling reek that seeps stinking out the street, marking the atmosphere: the passing of the cheese. Awful to admit to him! Like the hours before five a.m. Sooner say "I was up at ten past five" than admit to five to the hour. He is half four at best. A wet lowing lies somewhere at his origins. A reluctant cow was milked in the rain. Unpasteurized, clumsy, he free-ranges this city. He fetches up at your side and starts oozing. Cheese looks for kindness but gets the knife. Tie him up in a piece of gauze and be done.

CREATIVE WRITING LESSONS

I.   "Avoid the abstract and the general."

It is easy to avoid the abstract.
In the old days of powercuts and strikes,
I read books by candlelight.
Now at work we have the Internet
and I grow functionally illiterate:
sit through the hours of a long-haul flight
– as if; at my desk, almost pierrotized,
take bloodthinners, nor can read, nor write.
In the side of my left knee a small bird shrieks.
And it is the same thunder

There is no avoiding the general.
My mother is a little in love with him;
so must be the giants who hugged every wall
and his face rubbed off like a big heartprint.
Turn your back on the general, have your back to the wall –
His fascination makes scents. The general
has topnotes of mandarin, extraordinary sillage,
and a drydown of amber and bourgeoisie.
Back of my right nostril a black iris peers.
And it is the same thunder

II.   "Use the five senses to make things vivid and concrete."

–   Violence begins to enter this interchange.
–   I smash the decanted foreheads against the glass, insisting:
     "Look. Look outside."
–   Nothing shatters.
–   The landscape is colourful.

–   The deaf ones felt the music in the palms of their hands and
     the soles of their feet. They wept as they handed me an ice
     cream cone full of sand, which they had prepared because
     they thought me blind.

–   Two volunteered their answers to *touch*.
–   *Birds are sticky*, wrote the one who opened his fist, puzzled, in
     contemplation of the crushed down: the fledgling had known
     utter enclosure in the last moment before never achieving
     flight.
–   The other opened her mouth and began giggling as if against
     her will, as if she wished to speak, as if she also, all the time,
     had to run her own fingertips over her own fingertips, as if
     discovering fingerprints, as if that was it. I picked up the
     scissors and the intact doll she had let fall. I could smell the
     fledgling.

–   The transaction was as grotesque as if I had taken a handmade
     initialled silver tongue scraper to my fermented rice tongue to
     verify the residual no incremental fever of a kiss I had
     foregone.

–   In any case I was leafmeal dizzy with jasmine and unspeakable
     adhesives compounded by daily tramping the tarmac.

*She is vivid and concrete, on the whole, my sister. I have brought her in
as a teaching aid. Don't you like her? Come closer! Her hair is silky. Feel
it! It was perfumed from before her conception as her mother was confined*

31

for nine months to a bower carpeted with green herbs. Pick up her arm:
quiescent, just a little resistant. Don't you like her? Like her! Please! We
are one blood, she and I! And, for you, it's free
It's free

III. "Give evidence of process."

It comes out cramping
head like a blown lightbulb
I am supposed to love it
convince it of open meadows
there are none within miles to show it
feed it on toffee and clover
it grows up spitting and hitting out

Meantime my own child
I left under the flowerpot
I turn over the terracotta
discover two snakes

*

I SHOW YOU A MYSTERY

For Alex Houen

Such rain as could have fallen has fallen,
all the rain has gathered, an assumption
behind his eyes, a mineral entirety,
sufficient to derive the Kaieteur; rain,
blue tranquil flowerspike of illness;
a radiant containment; so much known;
such blue as nowhere else borne in one place.
The clear assumption gathers in his eyes.

Stand you said
        and standing I lay down
Here
    ·   six four o o kilometres
Listen
        clock in the macajuel gutter
I'm evening and you're night
and a spatter of rain
I have never seen such blue in one place.

As a survival artist puts in motion
(without witness) the steps of his evolution
towards winged posture (to his own hope and discomfiture)
relying on his paired, opposable skies –
As occasionally the tune changes,
the tune is charged with repetition
the body all spirit
air outrages fire
blue divorces green –
So too one iridescent birdflight
these extra, ordinary minutes
sunlight after rain.

When I shall have evolved and rain begins
again to finish falling, I expect
no change beyond diminished strangeness;
when, depth by depth, each room hammocks colour,
and the source of blue has gone to earth,
the rest is an assumption:
such blue: nowhere else.

CALLING TIME
For Emma Dillon

When he said *Look at the lakes*, I heard one thing with my head,
another with my body. It was a hot day. The talk
had been geological; only my feet were constant,
weeping blisters, statueified in Goretex. The whole way,
whatever we saw — plinth, plateau, ravine — his words effaced,
levelled, chiselled, explaining them in terms of something else;
waterfalls, modelled as once existing, would have rainbowed
the lakes — look.
   Dearest, do you remember not being drunk —
walking the strait line of sheer overwork, and the city
tilting? Well — Like that. I administered the narrow path
of my deep need.
   Somewhere below the ants, crow, cacti, changed
in the heat; the gently muscled water called attention;
I sat, and called time. Something rushing past forced my eyes shut.
So in purpleblack conscience of the quite empty blue sky
I figured an airplane collision. The lakes not looked at,
picking up cobalt, left their rock, ripple morphed to missile —
not underpowered renaissance arrows — direct, the hit
I'd feared, which would see me running out of myself; running
out, coming to an end; not looking where all waters go.
A hot day. There reigned a catastrophic indigo.

SUITE FOR ANTHONY MCNEILL

I.

whether if this were painting this line blue and white
would be quite clear crested the egrets heartstopping
the viewer's immediate lipswell handleaf drawn to kiss
the canvas skinprint to brushstroke were this a series of paintings
slided through breaklight cliché an anemometer paired with wings
i would gently as becomes a tribute roll down darkness
our fast night over the quite clear blue and white oh let it
so loveshaken the typist fluency forlorn
two-fingered punches holes in four-handed darkness
insistent that somewhere they're no longer shutting up the sun

II.

there's this poem i've not written
a photographer exhales
it comes within 3 days ¿what
comes? death comes within 3 days
of not drinking ¿not drinking
what? water… ssh, next door
he's asleep, the man who turned
into an iris; yes, smile;
so did he… whisper
unless you have forgotten
how to feel ¡that's risky! thirst…

III.

Encore de McNeill / south london railway station: six policemen throw down one sad loud man: we share a platform: *sushi sushi* public transport: take it away // Encore de McNeill / a man is smoking and he can't stop: he offered slopes to vines and little creatures: his fellows serve each other fingerbowls of molten molasses during slap-up meals of dirt: wisps of blues among the mudmen: volcano feathering his breast // Encore de McNeill / yellow rose infant adrift in a news café: dreaming in the arms of parents guilty as spain: moon in high flood in an open-shutters climate: two people face each other in a tidal room: dip north with the skies for a purple version of any of this // Encore de McNeill / fountain that won't turn off: green leaves snapping out from manuscript staves: a red dove carries one away: why did i fear you'd never write for us again: (do you read me?)

IV.

subject to sunbursts
the Pleiades fainted
single-star remix
when the face blossoms
the hands are shaking
open the guidebook
dried moss and violets
jump from the mouth
please identify them
you can talk to plants
so i have heard

V.

wasn't planned i'd write this poem
nude.
      being late
          to meet someone
i liked and hated
      for not being you
          for, not being you,
being possible.

cast off everything except
scarcity, thing we make ourselves:
      scarce:
          rhythm intervenes.
it happens so.

BOSPHORUS-STYLE STRAITS

drilling my lips (fish go swimming
grotesque as anything peaceful
journeying into hooks) apply shock's
high-grade sealant (unreflective
the freedom whose mouth falls open):
a different friend's said it again

don't tell anyone (cada noche)
(quoi?) may night glissade (tous les soirs?)
each night a catch-, slip-, -out, -up, anx-
iety stops here; first the sky,
weirdly inseminated, births squids
whence ink flashing like torpedos

when I look into your eyes,
always reflective *for how long
can you go on like this?* (to try
to think to try to think); a coin
for the woman cleaning the tiles,
please, bringing out the blue flowers...

GIFT OF A STAIRCASE
For Alice Yard

For the sake of clarity, which is the blackout, whaleback, salient and misguiding aspect of what I now hope to assay, I desire you to accept of me this staircase. I desire it for you in the diminishing of every association of staircase with birdcage. I desire you attentive to the unpicking of your own ribcage. I desire you vertiginous if you rise, if you walk, if you remain. I desire with you ascent.

Shaking off my old horrific procedure of careful omissions I would have burnt down the house except it fell upon itself, except it fell of itself, except I too needed to escape and did nothing and yet could not put myself out of the way of burning. You had begun the escape; why did I skirt the burning? We two may have escaped; what of the pervasive sensation of another burning? I am sensible of every blade of grass invisible by distance blocks away on lawns, fat green and purple crisped to a solar fury of worms. A surging somewhere, chromosomal, curlicues, unmendable. The destruction we both do and do not witness plumes sky-high and therefore appears entire and objective. So do we. So we do. Put from me this aspect, our doing, for there is this thing I now hope to assay.

I desire in yours my own assent.

In this blue-blue sky used to wheel a glory of vultures. What picked them off?

This is not a harp plundered along the journey of a grand piano's innards. This is not a mushroom's undercap wealth of soft dark spines. Oh yes, there is a family resemblance to the impressive wickerwork hand-plaited by our blind ones; but I've not brought you the gift of a chair.

Accept of me this staircase.

And that I too yearn skywards in the manifold increase of simplicity for which there is another name.

And that we look up hotly.

Oh you are lifted from me!

And about that which I left

unburnt

42

FOUR DEPARTURES FROM 'WULF AND EADWACER'

(i) reverse

It takes nothing from you that I have him —
    Bunched up in your ruins, you cannot lose.

He works alone.

Two sides of one city hide us.
Things fall apart, worked roads recoiling.
    Your lot would siphon grey from graveyards.
    Bunched up in your ruins, you cannot lose.

He works alone.

Near him I narrow to survival mode, wink out;
cannot say the time the place the mood,
hardly the aspect or the gender; again
we did nothing, we did nothing.

Could he for once be nobody's business —
    All too brightly meaningful
    ringbound dossiers flashing their backs,

I reach for the sleep he'd implanted in me;
turn my thorax inside out.

No pen and ink does it justice —
A Stanley knife lullaby score.

(ii) outside

"What was so lacking in the upbringing we gave her that she had to go off with a stranger, one of *them* as well; she's worthless, no getting her back, but so long as they're in touch with each other they're within our reach, for globalisation is also on our side. Their so-called love's as natural-seeming as the rain that falls with bitter charge, entering through the eardrums of our not-so-young houses to ancestral designs *he* only hopes to repossess. She's torn – it is transparent – about throwing in her lot with a fancy-passport foreigner whose hyena ways must make her sick. Best not lose sleep over prayers that her bastard will self-destruct in the womb, taking the mother to some lesser mansion in Heaven; never forget she is one of us, after all. A satisfactory solution will be found."

(iii) inside

If the present could be bloodier – can't imagine how.

    Dear Lord, I never intended this.

You were one kind of invasion, and another,
and it won't stop raining.

"I gave us all up?" To him. For him.

    Dear Lord, I never intended this.

We made notes only in mud or on pieces of wood
for burning, burnt; for cementing, trampled.
What can you hope to recover?
The nightjar stuck in my throat?

(iv) alpha@further.com

Eliminating all others from this poem save yourself, man, and what
made it worse, the brutality of your reception /well we have left a
misfit serenade, anachronistic whispers, slit of a wolf's eye into which
to post a brazen letter // ring around that // one comprehensive
guiltfear package presented via compressive anticipatory history //
ring around that // and if a wood were to turn on its own trees / hurt
by their individuality / and the seas rise up / in a perilous access of
island envy / and our coastal regions take sides about natural
processes / pitting churchmen against border guards against archi-
tects against weathering / could we make ourselves call what we have
/ a gift // one wanted or unwanted // I'd be first to destroy it, my bad
love, without doubt

FUSION

For Andre Bagoo

Fusion, meaning:
     burns behind eyelids
     capillaries' corals thickly
     foresting their otherwise rubies, diamonds, turquoises
     complicating the dark
     plugged into all sockets
     the seven hazardous mysteries
     shuttering compression of contacts
     the unremoved lens
     glass will grow again
     into the blasted cornea
     fusion, exacting its toll:
     colours it stole
     vowelling the moon fuchsia
     now snakes the crimson pathway, now the white
Fusion, meaning:
     laughing like you don't like it
     dreams go by contraries
     morning becomes electric
     having a passion that says teal

OF THE SAME METAL
After 'The Wife's Lament'
For Leila Capildeo

You hear?   She's off again.
A misery.
Say   I've been there too?
An ocean
asked longer   in those days
meant   the crossing,
what could be on board was different

screaming at wingtilt
would not bring on the shooting   just
surprise   pure
costing invisible   carbon unreckoned
deeply unmeasured
the clamber and sinking of oddities
undersea   I'm thinking
since I was caught

luminous as those   uselessly
evolved   unadaptable   lodged
in the conduit
shivered with crossfire
that family.

Any newcomer cut out
new channels for strife and grief.

Like an interpreter
he cleared off.

Drought yomped the gardens.
One day
fragrant   grateful
belonging to houses.

Next day
thrown down
the hardness of mountains
fires and thorns   who'd put
a door in that?   stow away
longlife goods   binding   muttering
lashing fast   labelling   finally
cowering
way beneath notice or the risk of news
without light
yet not out of reach of heat?

This makes you smile?
For your sheets are cooler
indeed you choose to keep them so?
Not singed   by dreams
while seeing off   each hour?
Lucky for true.
So often to turn back
not to turn back.

Till something   worse than no change

chance that
strikes   as cold as iron
as potentially magnetic
as likely to be equal in lethal or trivial use
as kind to handle
as sure to follow
below hearing level
susurration   filings
collecting as if escaping
patterning   obliquities
a field of likes

brings about
like us or not
an always.

*

JUST HOW HOT
After a UK weather report 1/vi/2011

"It's hotter than Africa.
In England, it's hotter than —"
"What! All of England —"
"It's hotter —"
"than all of — "
Africa! It's mainstream knowledge.
This summer, England's got the heat!
Google it; fold up your newspaper
to a cocked hat on a northface
mainstream lounger in excelsis
way above the vast dark sweatpatch,
the embarrassing continent;
count our pebbles — they've hatched, all gold!
Milk is turning in the bottles,
roses crying out to be (quick with it!)
distilled, taken off the branches;
our wasps are running marathons
intent perhaps on charity
in their veloce-veloce
(guess they do have them?) hearts;
this realm still better known as England
another implication of the sun —
jest
that
lie
back
and —
Put your tongue out if it's hotter than,
all of England, hotter than
Africa!
which I hear
can be a pretty cool place

PULL OUT ALL THE STOPS

Dear —,
I love you so much   I had to
write it somewhere   so
I am writing it
on the back of a receipt for apple strudel
in the British Museum café.
(There.
That feels better already).
Can you imagine
what you'd do to me in bed?
You could make me pay for
all the slights   the irritating
enigmas   the deliberate
inattention.   I hope so.
Make me pay   and pay again.
Like Dante
in that stony rhyming of his
desire to pin Beatrice down
twisting his fingers into her rope of hair
as she cries out through
all the hours   rung by
monks' bells   all through the long
medieval Tuscan day.
(Except
he never did).
You can't think   I'm up to constructing
another heaven?
I can't think   either.
This process of revision
final and   first touches!
I wrote this with my own hand:
Never let me go again   my love.

IDEAL VISITOR

The white rose looked in the mirror
and saw a skull.
I can't stay here, she decided.
So she moved on   spinosissima
welcome elsewhere
filled with the thorns of certitude.
Like a candle in a window
am I, she thought
for sure   and yet
in the steel framework and fragrance of night,
she terrorizes terraces:
plucking a downbeat to nod on
some glass of sleep   elegantissima
elicits screams:
dreamers wake jabbering of drought,
fields sweating salt to white beach-depth,
roads breaking up.
Murmurous with her own softness
the rose moves on   immaculatissima
belonging again and again
where an odour rises sharply,
lives lived without complexity
plead unawares
even in death for evening out death...

HYMN TO CERES, LONDON 2012

For Alex Houen

<london>
<spring> a thing of nothing </spring>
<spring> millstream wintergreen </spring>
<spring> null term in the 2050 glossary </spring>
<spring> veuillez expliciter </spring>
<spring> the mist returns </spring>
<spring> veuillez patienter </spring>
<spring> now the thing is </spring>
<spring> i start to miss you when I see you <<<
(margaretyoumournforerror 101)

London / seagulls encrypt a Boetti creation / white commas on kilims
of as they say oceanic and as eyes believe / heavenly / biro // mill'anni
e mille / victory to follow / blades r jumpin / n we take 2 the sky /
hardfastbrilliant / excepting the burst of birdstrike // Lyric Was Here
// the forensic guys deal with collectable remnants // oops / / our
feathered friends / oh how they flew till the day they were / snarge //

Do you have to mix it up? Write a song; it's time to sing…
One for the litterpicker the morning after. He knows
The rain; and rain, not always a poem, at least often
Falls softly on a labouring back… I dunno. Let him fix
His mark. His book. His city. Quick and still. Dew on bright foils.

ICE CREAM IN HYDE PARK WITH NIKKI
For Nikki Santilli

Time flies / she's a dancer / seagulls & eagles
we're watching walkers' & cyclists' ankles
straight up & down as posts! / larks & starlings
they ain't / that's Time / stopping & starting
singlescoop chocolatemint slipup
delicious / xylophonic strip / perfume-smelling forearms
vintage gardenia topnote soprano orangeblossom
she swoops / she sings / Time high-stepping
to her Lambretta scooter!
New York, hold your sidewalk breath

SHELL

For Jo Groiser

The sea needs no ornament.
She adorns herself with herself
and is herself our wreckage.
Unspontaneous as disbelief
the island combusting
– every sunset, despite the mist,
such mist, so very missed, chances
ourselves plunged in sunset
forever lying off the coast.
The railroad makes straight the house.
No names for you pass muster.
I wrote gods' names in the sand.

*

AFTER J.M.W. TURNER, *DEATH ON A PALE HORSE* (?)

Death, you're vain; incurable. I've not come here to harangue you,
having walked these galleries – I was sent on a quest by a lady, not to
feed your lack of inspiration.
You turn up smiling with your "Who? Me?" look, practically doing
a circus trick.
Less the rider of the famous pale horse than lying draped athwart its
foamy back like a battle-corpse of your own making ~~ the energy
with which the arms maintain ~ T-shaped ~ an absolutism of
posture ~ being a dead giveaway ~~~
C'est toi ~~~
Loose reins ~ invisible strings ~~~
You mean it ~~~
Does it have to be about you? You're sure?

A parachute could sooner be alive to its own silk, a magnolia to
suspense, a candelabrum to the Lord of Hosts – a lace collar likelier
to have conscience of its Puritan wearer, an archway to admonish a
grassblade, genitals to stop competing with cloud formations, and
contemplative arthritis to fetch up on a handy, masterpiece-fronting
bench – Any impossible could come to pass sooner than you come
to lose your conviction of your own centrality. Why do you think
you're stuck in a corner near a doorframe? To help you say hello?

You've insisted on tumult, appearing in storms of rust, bringing a
whirl of false charges against poets: that we're stalkers ~ venture into
your scorch zone ~ assault your patience ~ seek special treatment
~ want to get burnt ~ count blisters like gold rings ~ draw up a
siege in your field of excuses ~ scrape scarce meat from your shanks
for our stewpots ~ enmesh ourselves in your ribcage as if in cream
satin ribbons ~~~ We looked for you, so you reckon: lay in wait
at gateways where you'd flit out alone by preference ~ not a soul any
the wiser you'd been and gone ~~~
Though the deepest looks were yours into my eyes, I blame you
utterly.

The dead warned me about you. *All take and no give. What a performer.*
They are not in the picture. They are not on your side.

Is this really you? Riding for a fall? The cataloguers are unsure it's not
just some other horseman — I want it to be really you. So long as I can
tell rose from fire, love from sickness, word from dust. I am tender
of you.

Sole one to know what rest I need, and how much fatigue's ivoried
away in my bones. Inside out is how we're like each other. At last, too
much.
Dear generalist.
You glory from the wall. I stand here in my clothes
and additional, shivering dimensions.
Death...
You find yourself attractive most of all.

LORD OF CAVES

Shadow of birds crossed behind my closed eyes
Quadrant to quadrant pioneering nothing
Squadron to null   high peak to vanity
Formlessness they left me knowledge of grey

Snap this finger, sap comes out, I'm running
greenly, xylem and phloem support me.
Break a leaf off, souvenir to silence
now I grow roots not telling what a kill
you've made, oh lord, take a branch too, bleeding
no protest, what a laugh. Your hands run ash.

IMAGINARY FRIEND

You have the power to change times   disappear visibly.
I do not. Now   you say. Now. But how do you mean? I
tell you   time uses me through and through. If you look up
meditative as ever   from the fountain-pen curve
where metal drips ink (almost)   suddenly I'm on sand
trying to run towards Las Cuevas Bay   why   losing momentum
our flipflops sticking in the ooze   one foot rises free
and that is terrible   one stranded sandal   rapid
into quicksand masquerading as mud   gone like that.
Wait to want it back?   Day out   bite of the Atlantic
we're battling towards. Look. Take a minute from the shore.
My imaginary friend   why are you more than I
can hurry towards   finally   standing still?   Meet me
halfway   I was all too real.

TUSK

For Andre Bagoo

I.

Truthfully prone to brood a little
brooding apt to create a corner
creating an heap of mine enemies' skulls
they who earlier took cutlery round my brains
who, earlier having taken cutlery round my brains,
broke my fast grey wormlike processes
such that now I taste freedom, for the air
plays musical windows with my cranium
now here now there sunrise chairs in my dome
I have achieved such a polished presentation
oh as never before, you who are not my love,
purely incurred ivory transmitter glow;
you have a terrible memory, you who are not my love,
I am feeling to bowl along and bite you on the leg.

II.

What end these questions?
I see in the middle distance
a point: our acquaintance
where it maybe is cut

You in front I would be following leading
square steps to an avoidable plateau
stone basin of evisceration
where the sun no longer holds fire

Lizardflick incisions
overruning a wheel-less barrow
hip-height for presentation
an heap of literalized hearts

I see in the middle distance
mind cease   mine   mind's eye
mind seize   mine   mind sigh
mind's ease   mine   mind's aye

Who turns to face us?
Also I, proffering an apron
− I took them out over and over −
immobilizing hearts

III.

Brain
why demand
body running on water
why require
(lilac-winged)
the attentions (orange pollen under the tongue)
of sleep?

Line out of place
I disarranged it
wax on paintwork
I would not scrape it
light upon dust outlining
one size of shoe
no more

Talkative, the walls...
what are you celebrating?
floor, may you rejoice
in having been well fed
... yellowing the rosemary on the ledge
craves water
too cold...beggars eat heaped snow

Hands
lucky hands
in your expansile microclimate
assisting at your own flaying
you forget you cannot remember
you cannot know what you did not know
the anti-room's rotation, granular, in a black freeze

I turned the key in the door
and the dead soldiers
on the foldup ironing-board beds
turned a breath of welcome
and bells rang where the staircase has been removed
and I was made uneasy
by the formation of the here and now

Person of my last willing touch
intention darts, exits
via the backs of the fingers, via the ribs
reasserting extreme nowhere
leaving me standing
locked out of abstraction
weak as if in thaw

For happiness
a stonemason could substitute
five-petalled exactitude.
If not for you
if not for better listeners
– O gods who can be put out and not put out –
What is this thing I learn to do?

THE ULTIMATELY UNAVAILABLE HE

Caput Mortuum made love to me
in his imperious, frivolous way:
neither laying nor lifting a finger,
rather palming a heart
cutting out before tongue
un- and re-socketing eyes –
borrowed those time and again!
"It's the way you look –
You look so – I'd like to know –"
And now they don't quite work;
lifting them out with cleaned fingers
I laid them like devices with chargers
to bide sentencing in his head,
his douce and perdurable head.
I string myself along his teeth
dress a scaffolding to reach his cheeks
lean in to absence more tautly defined
than the voluptuous numquam of his mind:
for it is as I said
he is good and dead
I brought him to book
who'd take me as read

BUZZING OFF
For Peter Conrad

Put away the wings already folded in dust
and stop breathing. For this work is too engaging,
I have no allergies, I scent you through closed doors,
and your footfall brings nothing closer, by black light.

I sat on the rooftop and saw the trees rising
to wave goodbye. I saw the wave rising bluegreen.
An anxious fiddling inside the house was you
that kept inside inside. The waves rise blue-purple.

In the straight lines of the empire of workfriends
enthroned there sits one tiber-faced hands down hands down
handing down judgements! he likes you can play tigers,
an amusement is ground tigers, good medicine.

That intense quality only a wasp would have had
That incessant quality, only the sea;
To enter a chamber unstilled by musicking
now's a move to noise from noise, once was from silence

to

wings   scent   footfall   black light
trees   rising   inside   rising   waves
bluegreen   blue-purple   waves
straight lines, the empire
enthroned   handing   tigers
intense   incessant   only
too much, one too much
musicking   silence

now

A KIND OF DAWN

Fortunate World

I don't know what old is   if you are old.
Fortunate world
to know you longer than I could.

On Perpetual Alert

You know my mind   and do you know my heart?
You're on perpetual alert
a cruel time to be holding it.

Within

Moderate tea-drinker. "Water with berries in't"?
Severe caffeine within your persevering kiss
the imagined taste   perverse   I dreamt myself awake.

And

Delicate as who has held a flower
and no longer
trusts their fingers   grasp   my answer:

Spelled Distinct

Hard on the back of a fall I felt it
guessed it frost   feared   something that spelled
distinct rearrangement.

Half Myself

Getting up to go away I tore half
myself   tore off
nightfall   gritted the road you left.

A Kind of Dawn

When   helpful   yet still inadvertently
terrifying
when   springing with a smile   you frown

Who'd know to reckon that a kind of dawn?

SUNDAY

Someone carrying a beaker lost her footing.
Today's a mistake; however the sun hurries
to cover irregularities in the clouds,
the valley, that should be shallow, shows blue patches,
like lakes applied to a surface of peeled soil.
In this the houses are countable; the sheep, not...
In us the violence against them for standing
in clear shadow as if wetness were not, and noon
in clouds applied to hills as sheep outnumbering lamps.
The sheep knot; bellied, barely do anything but
sail in place; born tethered, they everywhere are free.
A figure on the ridge hurries towards them, slow
because far away, high up, slow because Sunday,
cyclonic mud underfoot, slow roast on the mind.

*

MONOLITHICITY
For Blofield Church, Norfolk

Knapped flint shines black. Flint's kind. Flint digged
from gravel pits   where flint has neighboured
iron may show red seepage.   Flint
sourced from near the sea is grey. Like all flint knapped
it shines black. Hand over hand over hand over
a hundred feet   pre-electronic labour   placed
(not meaning to expose)   this basic grimness   faced
the rough sides with strips of knapped and shining
flintwork.   The tower in a century
neared   completion.
Now is the tower of six hundred years ago.
You could see it as one. It rocks. The bellringers
knees over head   scapulas over head   all hands
over ropes in a lifethreatening lightening   feel this
as charted colour   number   sequence   as pulled peal
and in the sway of stone in wind. The tower rocks.
Do you think it was meant to? While the marguerites
make the white-capped ocean graveyard   meadow to
mast?

THERE IS A FIELD

Moaning and matting above and below ground
    grass spreads.
There is a field. There we may be together.
    Is it
pylons buzzing   laying hexes on our nearness
    air thrums
an electric abacus   invisible
    and spare
flesh counters static   fingers in their own fist
    stick   spark
tip of an index touching an earlobe hums
    this is
around us   there is a field. Where we may lie
    grass spreads.
Water resistance covers the soft of our feet
    and spare
water tames stalks of grain to beginning of –
    is it?
flooding from silted ditches though the ground's high
    air thrums
for the beginnings are binding together
    stick   spark
conductivity makes us its messengers
    this is
this field where together we form one lie
    grass spreads
like nervousness among collaborators
    air thrums
trimethylene   scent of decaying corpses
    and spare-
product fragrance in pagan hawthorn blossom
    (is it

sacrificial for that reason? smells like blood?)
    Stick   spark
civilization   lie to one side of what
    this is
Multiform   increasing its own distance   one
    grass spreads.
There is a field. We may have lain together.
    Is it
written we may not?   Voltage unmetred,
    air thrums
works us into the land's inclination   towers
    and spare
rebellion   climate lost to its overcoat
    stick   spark
imagining   It is not so grave. We lie?
    This is?

AS IN THE DESERT

This is the place where you come to a stone.
Search in the angles for a shadow of the stone.
Round and round you go   and you did not know
how harsh the loss of feeling in the feet can burn.
Oh all the cranes you have seen   the waterwings
plovers   cormorants   sandpipers   netting soft sky
rise off the thirst of the corpse you're making
it is you releasing shadows   water   and sky
reaching with softness for softness in stone.
How did you come to this place? They'd tell you better
histories   how it is marked as an oasis.
You don't look up. I'm telling you   this place is stone.
If I could reach down with you   a pebble
in the old watercourse   could start to pile a cairn

.   .   .

The bed dried up. The sand too hot to heap.
No small density to hand. You're beseeching stone
and what imaginary or legendary
travellers   what future comers   interpreters
would pick up the signals   if any could be made
after us? Desired as in the desert   water
of geographical tongues   valleyed   polyglot
studded from fire-eating   buds red oases
licks down stone   stone only seeming monolithic
stone made aghast its feather-mouth opens on shade

IN A DREAM

In what dream did I begin with you?
In what dream did I belong with you?
Every grey is edged with yellow,
this spit of narrow land is thrown
open between law and access,
the savage deliveries of sea.

One day I'll sleep   and that will be for a long time
and while I'm in a dream   all will have dream status
and while all's scheduled for dream   it will not matter
on the day of the longest dream   that you are part
in the dreaming   picking up where earlier glimpses
slipped painful perfections into which feet of sleep
walked   and as they walked   meadows began outspreading
slides of sleepscape   fourdimensional eyes of sleep
saw   and as they saw   you were there   more than spirit
easy   enduring   choosing our bodies' company
all the while you sang a trivial lyrical song
rhyming treasure   leisure   pausing to kiss and breathe
breathing being less required
Spirited away
I'll recall this sleep: reality. Like no dream
the years' complicated origami of hurt
in a dream   falling away   a puckered swan's fell
once blistered the maiden's skin inside   since   freely
tender to know   not to be urged to take   the air
dreaming   the false detachment of mornings cracked through
in its paper-lipped crudity of graph and talon   vivid line
grasping for its own excesses
One day of sleep the longest sleep and in a dream
so much will be suddenly unnecessary
shoes   when we're entering an ocean   obvious
for what has been obvious   our long-unseen dream

QUHEN
For Schir William Dunbar

[When] that I spelled and uttered your word's harsh start –
too young to understand – I told nobody that
you fetched up in my heart like a stalactite:
formed, formal, ruckled, fell;
struck through, I breathed you out,
nobody noticing you'd made me your kingdom,
in all the frozen variety of your freedom.
It was a little book, and I was six; it seemed
the size for me; the age difference, five centuries,
I couldn't reckon – nobody to tell. Besides,
your voice, its crackling paths, marked me a field for his –
You'd not foretold he would be beautiful to me,
and over the border of a murderous country.

TO SLEEP, POSSUM TO DREAM

possum descending a stairwell) a stepladder
numbers of sleep rounded up) possum defending
sealed caves of seal-sheep) sea-clouds) here merely daisies
) telling a petalled profusion of slumbering
possum) enamelled) possum logging out early
possum without compass seeks haystacks in haystacks
thorough innavigable cringly acres
impossumble n'est pas français a possum's nest
nest pas français a possum cantabile
possum untrainable) the nest unscheduled stop
the nest is silence) the deepest possumism
) opossum knows possum wakes only for possum
so accordingly all possumbilities hold...

THE JEWELLER AND THE WALLED GARDEN

I purposed roses, persuaded roses,
stayed roses past the season for roses,
spoke silks, stroked glass. The colour of kisses:
gold, best; black, worst; pink kisses, blue kisses,
blush and wisteria, very near best.
Rose though you are, you pass beyond roses.
Aflame, transforming, pure gold melts fast.

NIGHT IN THE GARDENS
For Sarah Simblet

I. Oxford and Port of Spain

The river murmurs.
On the instant all is flattened.
Nightfall conjures up the flood it is not.
Riding high   best survivors   the glass houses
somewhere to the east   containing reptile climates
floating leaves great as gongs able to support
one who'd wish to stand on water
if he's one of the cloud-skinned casually destructive kind
spinning a discus on one finger   stepping even
lighter than
lightly
illuminated you.
Rising high   buildings anxious as with knowledge
of new gravity   weigh light's felt outlines
as anxiety sharpens   even as sweat softens
the same set of features.
Known paths crackle towards some untoward paradise.
Buildings staying switched on yet not the destination
yellow   carries day unhurried nonetheless   inscapes
solar prolongation.
Dusken stone through inwardness knows itself awkward
as if larger   not yet spacious.
Nightfall conjures up its bluish straits   less than generous.

Refoliation murmurs all in all creating
two true weathers
one for fall watch one for storm alert.

II. Shield-Shaped

To bring a leaf of darkness
To bring a dusken leaf
The game how not to say it
Becoming not enough

Its back is ridged ensilvered
Its back is channelled code
For how it lived by moisture
And trembles with your blood

To hand it is to tear it
To hand one leaf is still
To scroll an ardent garden
Into your hand, I feel –

TITANIC

It is terrible – it is like death
and I do know death how I can know death:
alive,
some kinds of death:
for one,
putting these hands
to wet of a hole in this head
where was expected flesh,
watching these fingers, red,
come away with strands,
blood whose proteins strung a March dusk glittering
like Shakespeare says.
I proved his fancydress corpsekings
violent and plain.

It is not love-in-idleness, violet taste,
violet hour, the grey zone.

Choose a song
to sink to,
now the ships are down, the pines are sunk, the fish
bestraddle mountains;
now volcanoes kiss, with surprise, since æons undersea,
oxygen...

UTTER

First I tried to hide it from itself.
Then I tried to hide it from myself.
I tried quite hard to hide it from you,
even when we knew that was no use.
After all this hiding, no surprise
it's like a thing in translation:
eggshell-shy. A thumb's worth of glory,
nesting near the coastlines of your palm.

CONVERSATIONS FOR A LIFETIME
IN TWENTY MINUTES AND UNDER

two planes exited the runway of your face
my hands teared up and did not follow through

x

a wound that is also a thirst
a thirst that is also a river
a river that is also a consideration
a consideration that is also a cavern
a cavern of living saliva
there may we turn into snakes

x

deep awake in thought of you
it fetched some time to know
whose disembodiment
this was, and steady
out of such depth of sleep
smile to dream again

x

consider sleeping
sleep transient, sleep eternal,
sleep oblivious, sleep active,
sleep utterance, sleep walking,
sleep waking, sleep marriage,
the wooden cabin of you

x

when i met you   preparing
    meant to say   cleansed my body
    when i saw you   forgot my face
without home   remembering
    meant to write   a hundred strokes
    without whom   head upside down

x

would like to walk in a garden with you and hear the names of plants
that, as you call them, are all sensitive

x

seems so effortless
gods creating butterflies
you tying your scarf

x

citizenship
like being slapped about the face
that's your sunshine

x

home
so small
it exists
only when
i am not
in it
so small
i exist

only when
i'm contained
in it

x

every leaf bell star ever lyricized lives in your eyes

x

ceci n'est pas de la poésie d'amour, pretty
damn like it though a rose
is a rose is erosion

x

an impacted forest
extracted from birds
devastated only at our risk

x

my almost peaceful city, turn the other cheek

x

in all gentleness the cloud landed
and stayed halfway up the hillside
striking terror in my heart

x

ACKNOWLEDGEMENTS

Leila Capildeo & family; Andre Bagoo; Yvonne Berg; Christian Campbell; Ian Dieffenthaller; Anne Dillon; Emma Dillon; Anthony Esposito; Giles Goodland; Jo Groiser; Revd. Dr. Peter Groves; Nicki Heinen; Idara Hippolyte; Alex Houen; Maria Jastrzebska; Ágnes Lehóczky; Nicholas Laughlin; Vladimir Lucien; Karen Martinez; Rod Mengham; Inge Milfull; Kei Miller; Sharmistha Mohanty; Vivek Narayanan; Jeremy Noel-Tod & family; Ron Paste; Adam Piette; Deborah Price; Richard Price; Gemma Robinson & family; Nikki Santilli; Michael Scharf; Sisters of the Love of God, for solitude, company and sanctuary (Sr. Claire-Louise; Sr. Judith; Sr. Benedicta); Lucy Stone; Todd Swift; George Szirtes; John Hope Welch; John Whale; Courtenay Williams.

Poems have appeared in:
Caribbean Review of Books; *Exiled Writers Ink*; *Fence*; *Fire*; *The Oxford Magazine*; *Poetry Wales; Stand*; *Tate, Etc.*; *Tears in the Fence*

100 Poems from Trinidad and Tobago (Cane Arrow, 2013); *In Their Own Words: Contemporary Poets on their Poetry* (Salt, 2012); *Out of Bounds: British Black & Asian Poets* (Bloodaxe, 2012); *Sixty Poems for Haiti* (Cane Arrow, 2010); *The Best British Poetry 2012* (Salt, 2012); *Where We Fell to Earth: Writing for Peter Conrad* (privately printed, 2011)

Blackbox Manifold http://www.manifold.group.shef.ac.uk (Adam Piette; Alex Houen)
Town http://www.cometotown.blogspot.com (Nicholas Laughlin; Anu Lakhan)
The Lyre http://www.thelyreonline.blogspot.com (Ron Paste)
Pleasure http://pleasurett.blogspot.co.uk (Andre Bagoo)
Poetcasting http://www.poetcasting.org.uk (Alex Pryce)

ABOUT THE AUTHOR

Born in Port of Spain, Vahni Capildeo is the daughter of Leila Bissoondath Capildeo, who told her stories of East Trinidad, and the late Devendranath Capildeo, a poet. Capildeo's other formative influences include Indian diaspora culture (notably a preoccupation with boundaries between the human and the natural), French, and pre-1500 English literature. Capildeo read English Language and Literature at Christ Church, Oxford. Her awards (the Charles Oldham Shakespeare Prize; Viking Society Prize for Northern Research; Rhodes scholarship) reflect the intensity, variety and adventure of reading encouraged by the tutorial system. Shortly before her final examinations, she was struck by a speeding police car. During her convalescence, she could not read. At this time, she formed the friendship with medieval musicologist Emma Dillon which led to an enduring interest in the musical possibilities of poetry and prose. While remaining at Christ Church to work on a doctorate in Old Norse and translation, Capildeo had her first poems published in student magazines such as Jeremy Noel-Tod's *Zero*. During this period, she completed and destroyed a first poetry manuscript. Capildeo subsequently won a Research Fellowship at Girton College, Cambridge. The inspirational leadership of Professor Dame Marilyn Strathern allowed Capildeo to intermit and spend essential months immersed in the cultural and family environments of Trinidad and Jamaica. This led to Capildeo's first book, *No Traveller Returns* (Salt, 2003) and the draft of her dramatic pamphlet *Person Animal Figure* (Landfill, 2005). Despite her preference for non-academic professional roles, Capildeo has worked for the universities of Glasgow, Leeds, Sheffield, Kingston-upon-Thames and Greenwich. She is grateful for the poetic guidance of Professor John Whale and the conversations with a brilliant set of students while she held a Teaching Fellowship in Creative Writing at the University of Leeds. The landscapes of Yorkshire can be found in her second book, *Undraining Sea* (Egg Box, 2009), which was Highly Commended for the Forward Prize (individual poem category, 2009) and shortlisted for the Guyana International Prize for Literature (2011). The

University of Sheffield introduced two more important creative friendships to Capildeo's life: with Professor Adam Piette and Dr. Alex Houen, editors of the innovative e-zine *Blackbox Manifold*, for which Capildeo is a contributing advisor. Capildeo enjoys collaborating with artists from other disciplines, co-creating performances with the Oxford Improvisers and the DEC Collective, and working with Andre Bagoo on a text/image project on urban decay in Trinidad, recorded in the art book *Disappearing Houses* (Alice Yard, 2011). Capildeo is a keen writer of prose as well as poetry. Her unpublished memoir, *One Scattered Skeleton*, was chosen by UK blogger and journalist Ann Morgan as Trinidad's representative book in the 'Year of Reading the World' project: http://ayearofreadingtheworld.com/tag/vahni-capildeo/ Her work in various genres has been widely anthologized, for example in Iain Sinclair's *London: City of Disappearances* (Penguin, 2006) and *Trinidad Noir* (Akashic, 2008). Like *Utter*, Capildeo's most recent book, *Dark & Unaccustomed Words* (Egg Box, 2012; shortlisted for the OCM Bocas Poetry Prize) was inspired by her time working in the Etymology Group and the Research Group at the Oxford English Dictionary. Capildeo's volunteer roles at Oxfam Head Office and the Oxford Sexual Abuse and Rape Crisis Centre helped prepare her for her current position as Programme Officer with the Commonwealth Writers' Team at the Commonwealth Foundation.